Energy for Today

Nuclear Power

By Tea Benduhn

Reading consultant: Susan Nations, M.Ed.,
author/literacy coach/consultant in literacy development

Science and curriculum consultant: Debra Voege, M.A.,
science curriculum resource teacher

WEEKLY READER®
PUBLISHING

Please visit our web site at www.garethstevens.com.
For a free color catalog describing our list of high-quality books,
call 1-800-542-2595 (USA) or 1-800-387-3178 (Canada). Our fax: 1-877-542-2596

Library of Congress Cataloging-in-Publication Data

Benduhn, Tea.
    Nuclear power / by Tea Benduhn.
       p. cm. — (Energy for today)
      Includes bibliographical references and index.
      ISBN-10: 0-8368-9262-3 — ISBN-13: 978-0-8368-9262-8 (lib. bdg.)
      ISBN-10: 0-8368-9361-1 — ISBN-13: 978-0-8368-9361-8 (softcover)
      1. Nuclear energy—Juvenile literature. I. Title.
  TK9148.B46 2009
  621.48'3—dc22   2008012020

This edition first published in 2009 by
Weekly Reader® Books
An Imprint of Gareth Stevens Publishing
1 Reader's Digest Road
Pleasantville, NY 10570-7000 USA

Copyright © 2009 by Gareth Stevens, Inc.

Senior Managing Editor: Lisa M. Herrington
Senior Editor: Brian Fitzgerald
Creative Director: Lisa Donovan
Designer: Ken Crossland
Photo Researcher: Diane Laska-Swanke

Image credits: Cover and title page: © Christopher and Sally Gable/Getty Images; p. 5: SOHO (ESA & NASA);
p. 6: © Creatas Images/Jupiterimages Unlimited; p. 7: © Comstock Images/Jupiterimages Unlimited; p. 9: © Kyle
Smith/Shutterstock; p. 10: © Martin Bond/Photo Researchers, Inc.; p. 11: © John Sohlden/Visuals Unlimited; p. 12:
© Medioimages/Photodisc/Getty Images; p. 14: © Jacana/Photo Researchers, Inc.; p. 15: © Jean Louis Batt/Getty
Images; p. 16: © U.S. Department of Energy/Photo Researchers, Inc.; p. 18: © allOver photography/Alamy; p. 19:
© vladphotos/Alamy; p. 20: © Jim West/Alamy; p. 21: © Julie Alissi/Weekly Reader.

Printed in the United States

1 2 3 4 5 6 7 8 9 10 09 08

Table of Contents

Words that appear in the glossary are printed in **boldface** type the first time they occur in the text.

Chapter 1

What Is Nuclear Power?

Do you enjoy watching television or playing video games? Have you eaten food cooked in a microwave? Do you often flip a switch to turn on a light? All of these activities use electricity. Electricity is a form of **energy**. We use energy from water, wind, and the Sun to make electricity. Nuclear power is another form of energy we use to make electricity.

Nuclear power makes the Sun give off light and heat.

Nuclear power comes from **atoms**. Atoms are so small that we cannot see them. If people were the same size as atoms, everyone in the world could fit on the point of a pin! Atoms make up everything in the universe. People, pins, and the Sun are all made of atoms. The Sun shines because of nuclear power.

Atoms are tiny, but they have huge amounts of energy. Energy can change from one form to another. **Potential energy** is stored. Objects in motion have **kinetic energy**. When you sit at the top of a slide, you have potential energy. When you move down the slide, your energy changes to kinetic energy. The potential energy in atoms changes to kinetic energy when atoms are broken apart.

Do you see potential energy or kinetic energy in this photo?

When you knock down dominoes, you are making a chain reaction.

Scientists use a **chain reaction** to break apart atoms. You see a chain reaction when you knock down rows of dominoes. If you knock down one domino, it knocks down the next. Each domino knocks down the next one in line. The atoms in a chain reaction are like dominoes. When one atom splits, it hits another atom and breaks it apart and so on.

Chapter 2

Sources of Energy

We get energy from different sources. Most of our energy comes from oil, gas, and coal. Oil, gas, and coal are **fossil fuels**. They come from the remains of plants and animals that lived millions of years ago. Fossil fuels are **nonrenewable resources**. Once they are used up, they are gone forever.

We burn fossil fuels to make energy. Burning fossil fuels lets off heat. It also makes **pollution**. Polluted air is hard to breathe. Polluted water can make people and animals sick. Scientists say gases from burning fossil fuels are causing Earth to slowly heat up. This worldwide rise in temperature is called **global warming**.

Power plants that burn coal for energy also make air pollution.

Some energy sources do not cause pollution. Clean energy often comes from **renewable resources**. The Sun, water, and wind are clean energy sources. They are also renewable resources. We will not run out of them after they are used for energy.

Wind is a renewable source of energy. Wind farms make electricity.

Nuclear power does not let off air pollution. It also does not give off the gases that cause global warming. Nuclear power comes from nonrenewable resources, however. The atoms used to make nuclear power come from **uranium**, a metal found in many rocks. After uranium is used to make energy, it cannot be used again.

Nuclear power does not let off air pollution. The "smoke" rising from the towers is a gas called water vapor.

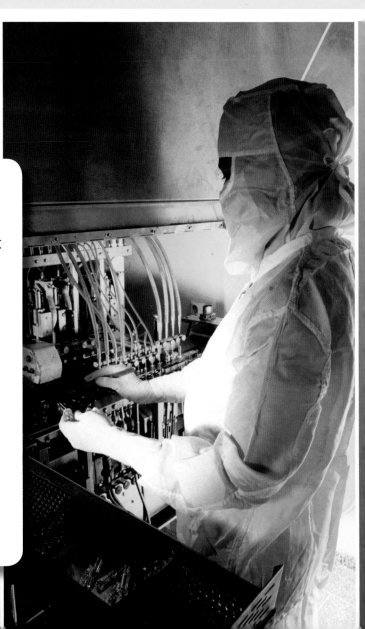

Workers at nuclear power plants wear special suits to protect them from radiation.

Nuclear power lets off heat, just as fossil fuels do. Scientists use this heat to make energy. Heat is a type of **radiation**. Radiation is all around us. Light is another type of radiation. Some radiation given off by nuclear power plants is dangerous. Nuclear radiation can kill people and animals. Scientists must be careful when they work with nuclear power.

Chapter 3

How Nuclear Power Works

There are two ways to get energy from an atom. The Sun makes energy by pushing atoms together to make bigger atoms. Atoms give off energy when they get bigger. Splitting atoms apart is another way to release energy. The process of splitting apart atoms is called **fission**. Fission makes atoms smaller. Atoms give off energy when they break apart.

Uranium atoms can break apart easily. When the atoms break, they let out energy stored inside. Scientists use uranium pellets in nuclear power plants to make energy. Each pellet of uranium is about the size of a jellybean. Uranium makes more energy than fossil fuels do. A single pellet has as much energy as 150 gallons (568 liters) of oil!

Scientists get uranium from some types of rocks.

If you could see atoms, nuclear fission might look like a game of marbles.

Think of splitting atoms as marbles. If you shoot one marble into a group, it starts a chain reaction. The marbles scatter in different directions. They roll into other groups of marbles. Nuclear energy works in a similar way. One atom crashes into another atom and splits it apart. Each splitting atom hits other atoms. The chain reaction of splitting atoms gives off huge amounts of energy.

In a nuclear reactor, fission takes place underwater.

The nuclear chain reaction happens inside a machine called a **nuclear reactor**. When uranium atoms break apart, they let off heat. Scientists use this heat to make energy. The heat boils water to make steam. The steam spins a **turbine**. When turbines turn, they create electricity.

Chapter 4

Nuclear Power in the Future

Every year people use more electricity. Around the world, people use more fossil fuels for energy. Fossil fuels will run out someday. Scientists are making other sources of energy more available. Today, about 20 percent of the electricity in the United States comes from nuclear power.

Some people are afraid of nuclear power, however. They worry about radiation leaking out of a power plant and making them sick. Scientists are very careful when they build nuclear reactors. They make sure to protect people from radiation. They build thick concrete walls to block radiation from leaking out.

The nuclear reactor is inside a concrete dome. Its thick walls would hold in radiation that leaked during an accident.

This classroom near Chernobyl, Ukraine, has been empty for more than 20 years. The area is still unsafe.

Nuclear power can be dangerous. As with any energy source, people must be very careful when using it. In 1986, fuel melted in a nuclear power plant in Chernobyl, Ukraine. The power plant was damaged. Radiation spread across Europe. Thousands of people got sick or died. Today, few people live within 19 miles (30 kilometers) of Chernobyl because it is still too dangerous.

Although nuclear power does not make air pollution, it does make dangerous nuclear waste. The waste can last for thousands of years. Scientists seal nuclear waste in thick steel or concrete containers. Over time, the steel or concrete can break down. Scientists are working on ways to store the waste more safely. The U.S. government plans to bury its nuclear waste deep underground in Yucca Mountain, Nevada.

Workers inspect a tunnel under Yucca Mountain, Nevada. The U.S. government plans to bury nuclear waste under the mountain.

Nuclear power cannot answer all of our energy needs. In the future, we will need to use other energy sources. We must **conserve**, or save, energy, too. To save energy, we can turn off lights when we leave a room. In summer, we can open windows instead of using air conditioning. What are some other ways you and your family can save energy?

Glossary

atoms: tiny particles that make up all matter

chain reaction: a series of events that are all set off by one thing

conserve: to save

energy: the ability to do work

fission: the breaking apart of atoms to release energy

fossil fuels: sources of energy, such as oil, gas, and coal, that formed from the remains of plants or animals that lived millions of years ago

global warming: the slow rise in Earth's temperature

kinetic energy: energy that is moving

nonrenewable resource: a resource that cannot be used again. Once it is used, it is gone forever. Fossil fuels are nonrenewable resources.

nuclear reactor: a machine that makes nuclear power

pollution: harmful materials in the environment

potential energy: energy that is stored

radiation: rays or waves that are let off by a nuclear reaction

renewable resource: a resource that can be used again. Renewable resources include air, water, sunlight, wind, and plants and animals.

turbine: a machine that turns to create electricity

uranium: a metal that is used to make nuclear power

To Find Out More

Books

Atoms. Simply Science (series). Melissa Stewart (Compass Point Books, 2003)

Nuclear Power. Sources of Energy (series). Diane Gibson (Smart Apple Media, 2004)

Web Sites

Kaboom! Energy

tiki.oneworld.net/energy/energy.html
Learn about many sources of energy, including nuclear power.

Nuclear World

www.aecl.ca/kidszone/atomicenergy/nuclear
Watch an animated clip of nuclear fission.

Publisher's note to educators and parents: Our editors have carefully reviewed these web sites to ensure that they are suitable for children. Many web sites change frequently, however, and we cannot guarantee that a site's future contents will continue to meet our high standards of quality and educational value. Be advised that children should be closely supervised whenever they access the Internet.

Index

About the Author

Tea Benduhn writes books and edits a magazine. She lives in the beautiful state of Wisconsin with her husband and two cats. The walls of their home are lined with bookshelves filled with books. Tea says, "I read every day. It is more fun than watching television!"